Best Joke Book Ever

Charles Keller

Illustrated by Jeff Sinclair

Sterling Publishing Co., Inc.
New York

To Gabriel

Library of Congress Cataloging-in-Publication Data

Keller, Charles.
   Best joke book ever / Charles Keller ; illustrated by Jeff Sinclair
     p. cm.
   Includes index.
   ISBN 0-8069-9865-2
   1. American wit and humor. I. Sinclair, Jeff. II. Title.
   PN6162.K44 1998
   818'.5402–dc21   97-48902
                                         CIP

10 9 8 7 6 5 4 3 2

First paperback edition published in 1999 by
Sterling Publishing Company, Inc.
387 Park Avenue South, New York, N.Y. 10016
© 1998 by Charles Keller
Illustrations © 1998 by Jeff Sinclair
Distributed in Canada by Sterling Publishing
% Canadian Manda Group, One Atlantic Avenue, Suite 105
Toronto, Ontario, Canada M6K 3E7
Distributed in Great Britain and Europe by Chris Lloyd
463 Ashley Road, Parkstone Poole, Dorset BH14 0AX, England
Distributed in Australia by Capricorn Link (Australia) Pty Ltd.
P.O. Box 6651, Baulkham Hills, Business Centre, NSW 2153, Australia
Manufactured in the United States of America
All rights reserved

Sterling ISBN 0-8069-9865-2 Trade
                0-8069-9870-9 Paper

Contents

1. Happy Days

BOY: Little Joey finally ate his oatmeal.
MOTHER: How did you get him to eat it?
BOY: I told him it was mud.

I've tried making an upside-down cake.
   How did it turn out?
It was a complete flop.

Try this sponge cake. I made it myself.
   It's a little tough.
I can't understand why. I made it from a fresh
sponge.

Why are you eating your dinner on the side of the street?

The doctor told me to curb my appetite.

DOCTOR: The best thing for you is to give up sweets, fatty foods, smoking and drinking.

PATIENT: What's the second best?

BOOKS NEVER WRITTEN

Is Your Family Well? by Howard D. Folks.

Dental Examination by Hope N. Wide.

The Broken Window Mystery by Eva Brick.

Choosing a Pet Bird by Perry Keat.

VETERINARIAN: Nurse, why are there 101 Dalmatians in the office?

NURSE: They all have the same problem. They keep seeing spots before their eyes.

I can pick up a cent with only two fingers.

That's nothing. My dog can do it with its nose.

I just built this great big doghouse for my dog.

Big deal, my turtle came with his own.

How do you like my new swimming pool?
It's nice, but why is there no water in it?
Because I can't swim.

Why did the writer enjoy working in the basement?
Why?
He was writing a best cellar.

POET: Do you think I should put more fire in my
poetry?
PUBLISHER: No, I think you should put more poetry
in the fire.

I picked up an encyclopedia at a garage sale.
*You only have four volumes. How could you pick up an
encyclopedia with books missing?*
I don't have to know everything.

BOSS: How is it that every time I come around
you're not working?
WORKER: You wear sneakers.

LADY: Can I wear these leather shoes in the rain?
CLERK: Did you ever see a cow carrying an
umbrella?

Did you hear about the fire at the shoe factory
when over a thousand soles were lost?

LITTLE BROTHER: I'm going out to water the flowers.
BIG BROTHER: But it's raining!
LITTLE BROTHER: That's okay. I'll wear my raincoat.

There's no water in the can you're going to water
the flowers with.

That's okay. They're artificial flowers.

LADY: What should I plant if I want pastel-colored
flowers?

GARDENER: Light bulbs.

What kind of plant is that?

It belongs to the dahlia family.

Oh, I thought it was yours.

Look at the beautiful bunch of roses I got for my
girlfriend.

Wow! How did you make a trade like that?

BOY: May I see you pretty soon?
GIRL: Why? Don't you think I'm pretty now?

What do you mean our financial situation is fluid?
We're going down the drain.

The bank returned your check.
Good, now I can use it for something else.

BANK: I'm afraid your checking account is
overdrawn.
MAN: That's impossible. I still have five checks left.

Remember last year when I was broke and you
helped me and I said I'd never forget you?
Yes, I remember.
Well, I'm broke again.

What's that on your wrist?
It's a memory band.
What's it for?
I forgot.

I've got this great new watch. It tells the date, the
weather and your horoscope. There's only one
thing it can't do.
What's that?
Tell time.

Why do you always wear two watches?
I need one to see how fast the other is.

BOOKS NEVER WRITTEN

Getting There on Time by Harriet Upp.

How to Be Different by Y.B. Normal.

I Was a Double Agent by Espy N. Odge

Driving an R.V. by Winnie Bago

I woke up last night with the feeling my watch was gone.

Was it gone?

No, but it was going.

WOMAN: Is your taxicab engaged?
CAB DRIVER: No, but it's going steady.

TAXI DRIVER: I can't stop this car! I've lost control!
PASSENGER: For heaven's sake! Turn off the meter!

TAXI DRIVER: I forgot to turn the meter on, so I don't know how much to charge you.
PASSENGER: That's okay. I forgot to bring money, so I wasn't going to pay you anyway.

CAB DRIVER: Lady, that 25-cent tip you gave me was an insult.
LADY: How much should I tip you?
CABBIE: Another 25 cents.
LADY: I wouldn't think of insulting you twice.

2. Let the Good Times Roll

Don't forget to bring home another mouse trap.
What's the matter with the one I bought yesterday?
It's full.

BOY: Mister, could you sell me a shark?
PET SHOP OWNER: What would you do with a shark?
BOY: The cat's trying to eat my goldfish and I want
to teach him a lesson.

What's your cat's name?
It's Santa. But don't pick it up.
Why not?
Because Santa claws.

My cat's head has been drooping. I'm taking him to a vet.

Neck's weak?

No, tomorrow.

LION: Let's get something to eat. Let's go after that hair stylist.

OTHER LION: I can't eat him. He's my mane man.

Did you hear about the hair stylist who got rid of her boyfriend by giving him the brush?

How many times have I told you not to be late for dinner?

I don't know. I didn't think you were keeping score.

CUSTOMER: Waiter, there's a twig in my soup.
WAITER: That's no surprise, we have branches everywhere.

A string bean took his friend, a pea, to the hospital.
STRING BEAN: How is he, doc? Can you save his life?
DOCTOR: I have good news and bad news. The good news is I can save his life. The bad news is he'll be a vegetable the rest of his life.

PATIENT: Nurse, during the operation I heard the doctor say a four-letter word that upset me very much.
NURSE: What was the word?
PATIENT: Oops!

DOCTOR: Congratulations! You're the father of twins.
MAN: Don't tell my wife. I want to surprise her.

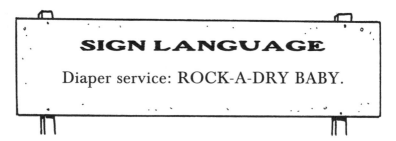

SIGN LANGUAGE

Diaper service: ROCK-A-DRY BABY.

We got a new brother at my house.
Really? Where did you get him?
From Dr. Klein.
No kidding. We take from him too.

How old is your baby sister?
She's last year's model.

Where do you live?
On Minute Street.
I never heard of Minute Street.
That's because most people call it 62nd Street.

PASSERBY: I see you're building a new house.
BUILDER: Yes. That's the only kind we build.

DAFFYNITIONS

Wholesale—Where a mouse goes to buy a house.

Delighted—When the light bulb in your room is burned out.

Thuds—What happens when the thoap gets wet.

Childhood—a young gangster.

POLICEMAN: Do you know that's a stolen car you're driving?
DRIVER: Of course I do. How do you think I got it?

GRANDFATHER: Uh, oh! I just made an illegal right turn.
GRANDSON: That's okay, Grandpa. The police car behind you did the same thing.

TRAFFIC COP: Your license says you should be wearing glasses. Why aren't you wearing them?
MOTORIST: I have contacts.
COP: I don't care who you know. I'm giving you a ticket.

Did you hear about the new car that runs on peanut butter? It gets good mileage but sticks to the roof of your garage.

BABY CANNIBAL: Mom, what are we having for lunch?
MOTHER CANNIBAL: Ladyfingers.

FIRST CANNIBAL: Am I late for dinner?
SECOND CANNIBAL: Yes, everyone's eaten.

MOTHER: Didn't I ask you to notice when the soup boiled over?
DAUGHTER: I did, Mom. It was at 7:30.

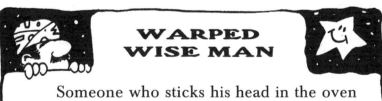

WARPED WISE MAN

Someone who sticks his head in the oven will end up with a baked bean.

What do you call a guy who eats meat, vegetables and potatoes?
   What?
Stu.

Did you hear about the corn that got into a fight and got creamed?

FARMER: Would you like to take this chicken home to eat?
CITY SLICKER: I would. But what would I feed him?

Why did Mozart sell his chickens?
  I'm not sure, why?
They ran around saying, "Bach, Bach, Bach."

FARMER: I have the laziest rooster in the country.
OTHER FARMER: Why do you say that?
FIRST FARMER: When the sun comes up, he never crows. He waits until the others crow, and then he nods his head.

My uncle is an umpire in a restaurant.
  What does he do?
When someone orders pancakes he yells, "Batter up."

What does an umpire do when he gets a headache?
  I don't know. What?
Takes two aspirins and calls as little as possible.

Do you really like baseball?
  Sure, don't you?
Not anymore.
  Why not?
Every time I get to third base the coach tells me to go home.

3. Fun Time

HUSBAND: I've got to hire a new chauffeur. He nearly killed me today.

WIFE: Oh, give him another chance.

LADY: I need a present for my husband.

SALESMAN: How about a smoking jacket?

LADY: He doesn't smoke.

SALESMAN: Then how about a hunting jacket?

LADY: He doesn't hunt.

SALESMAN: You can't turn down a bathrobe, can you?

Do you always bathe in muddy water?

It wasn't muddy when I got in.

MOTHER: I have just drawn you a bath.
SON: I get the picture.

That joke was so old when I first heard it, the Dead Sea was only sick.

A vampire took an ocean cruise. He went into the dining room and said, "I'm starving."

"Would you like to see a menu?" said the waiter.

"No," answered the vampire. "Just bring me the passenger list."

FIRST MONSTER: We must be getting close to the city.
SECOND MONSTER: Why do you think that?
FIRST MONSTER: We're stepping on more people.

FIRST DRAGON: Do you breathe fire?

SECOND DRAGON: Nope, not since I stopped smoking.

What did the ghost name its new motel?
What?
Rest Inn Peace.

TRAVELER: I'd like a room.

HOTEL CLERK: With a tub or a shower?

TRAVELER: What's the difference?

CLERK: You sit down in a tub.

HOTEL OWNER: I won't charge you for the breakfast because you didn't eat it.

GUEST: Thanks. By the way, I didn't sleep last night.

MAN AT HOTEL: Excuse me, but I'm registered at this hotel. Could you tell me what room I'm in?

HOTEL CLERK: Certainly, you're in the lobby.

BOSS: What's this big item on your expense account?

SALESMAN: Oh, that's the hotel bill.

BOSS: Well, don't buy any more hotels.

WORKER: My wife says I should ask you for a raise.

BOSS: I'll ask my wife if I can give you one.

EMPLOYEE: I've worked here for over 30 years and I have never asked for a raise.

BOSS: That's why you've worked here for 30 years.

I finally got my boss to laugh.
Did you tell him a joke?
No, I asked for a raise.

NEWS BULLETIN

A woman was fired from her job at
the lingerie shop and was given the pink slip.

I got fired from my last job because I was too
tough.
What do you mean?
I didn't take orders from anybody.

TOM SWIFTIES

"What was I supposed to buy?" asked Tom
listlessly.

"I guess I'll have to change the light bulb," said
Tom dimly.

"It smells like gasoline in here," Tom fumed.

"Step on the brakes!" Tom screeched.

SIGN LANGUAGE

Sign in a muffler shop: NO APPOINTMENT NECESSARY. WE HEARD YOU COMING.

I have this terrible problem. Whenever I go shopping I buy everything that is marked down.
Why is that a problem?
Last week I bought an escalator.

CUSTOMER: I can't find words to express my annoyance.
STORE CLERK: May I sell you a dictionary?

SALESMAN: You make a small down payment and then you don't make any more payments for six months.
CUSTOMER: Who told you about me?

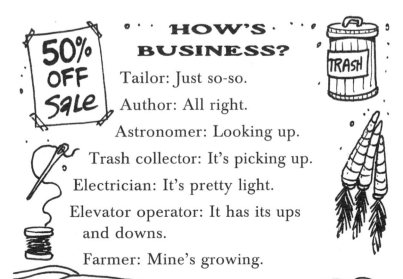

HOW'S BUSINESS?

Tailor: Just so-so.

Author: All right.

Astronomer: Looking up.

Trash collector: It's picking up.

Electrician: It's pretty light.

Elevator operator: It has its ups and downs.

Farmer: Mine's growing.

When I bought this car you guaranteed you'd fix anything that broke.

Yes, sir.

Then I want a new garage.

MAN: How much is that compact model?

CAR SALESMAN: $15,000.

MAN: That's as much as a big car.

CAR SALESMAN: Well, if you want economy you have to pay for it.

FARMER: Let me explain farming to you. First we raise corn. If a good crop comes up then we raise wheat.

CITY SLICKER: What if a good crop doesn't come up?

FARMER: Then we raise prices.

FARMER: Tell me, Zeke, do you have a watermelon patch?

ZEKE: Why, do you have a leaking watermelon?

CITY BOY: Can I cut across your field so I can make the 10 A.M. train?

FARMER: Sure, but if my bull sees you, you'll make the 9 A.M. train.

YOUNG MAN: Help! My father is being chased by a bull.

SHOPKEEPER: What can I do?

YOUNG MAN: Get me some film for my camera.

FIRST RANCHER: I have 100 horses.

SECOND RANCHER: I have over 200 head of cattle.

THIRD RANCHER: I don't want to brag, but my herd of sheep is so big, every time I try counting them I fall asleep.

DAFFYNITIONS

Bacteria—The rear entrance to a cafeteria.

Diet—A question of mind over platter.

Dieting—Penalty for exceeding the feed limit.

Birdhouse—Home tweet home.

Are you milking that cow in your new hat?
No, I'm using a pail.

A farmer showed a city boy a large cow. "They give us whole milk."
Don't you have any skinny cows?
Why?
For skim milk.

What do you do when your mother gives you money for a Popsicle?
Ice cream.

23

I'm thirsty.
I'm Friday. Come over on Saturday and we'll have a sundae.

BIRD WATCHER: That bird has the wisest eyes and that one has the strongest claws.
STUDENT: I guess that one must be the shopping bird. It has the biggest bill.

MOTHER PIGEON: It's time you learned to fly. Either you learn or I'll tie a rope to you and tow you.
YOUNG PIGEON: Oh, no, not that! I'd rather die than be pigeon towed.

I'm glad I'm not a bird.
Why?
Because I can't fly.

4. Clowning Around

BANK PRESIDENT: Do you know where the cashier is?

ASSISTANT: He went to the race track.

PRESIDENT: During working hours?

ASSISTANT: He said it was the last chance to balance the books.

Do elephants know how to gamble?
I don't have the Vegas idea.

More than 50,000 elephants go each year to make piano keys.

Really? It's amazing what animals can be trained to do these days.

CUSTOMER: I'd like to buy a piano. Does it come with a guarantee?
SALESMAN: Yes, I guarantee it's a piano.

Son, I think you should wash your hands. The piano teacher is coming here in 10 minutes.

Don't worry, Mom, I'll only play the black keys.

MOTHER: Did you fall down with your good pants on?
SON: Yes, I didn't have time to take them off.

MOTHER: Did you sweep behind the door?
DAUGHTER: I swept everything behind the door.

Sometimes I think you don't hear a word I say.

What?

FATHER: Where's today's newspaper?
SON: I threw it out with the garbage.
FATHER: I wanted to see it.
SON: There wasn't much to see. Some chicken bones, a banana peel and some coffee grounds.

NEWSPAPER OFFICE: City desk, speaking.
CALLER: Really! What drawer?

CUSTOMER: How much does your newspaper charge for funeral notices?

NEWSPAPER CLERK: Two dollars an inch.

CUSTOMER: Wow! My uncle was six-foot-four.

What are you doing with that rope?
  I'm committing suicide.
Why do you have the rope around your waist?
  When I put it around my neck I can't breathe.

Did you hear about the 100-year-old man who just died?
  No, what did he finally die of?
Blowing out the candles on his birthday cake.

PERVERTED PROVERB

A fool and his money are invited everywhere.

Did you know that Eskimos once used fish for money?
Gee, I'll bet they had a hard time getting a can of soda out of the machine.

How come you go fishing every day?
I can't help it. I'm hooked.

Have you caught any fish yet?
No, I think my worm isn't trying.

Mom, there's a man at the door with a package marked C.O.D.
Sounds fishy to me.

What are those things floating in the water?
Jellyfish.
What flavor?

Is that a surfboard?
No, it's a tongue depressor for my pet shark.

On the ocean they use knots instead of miles.
Why the difference?
Because they have to keep the ocean tide.

Wanna go to the beach?
Shore.

I was once a 90-pound weakling. When I went to
the beach some 200-pound bully kicked sand in my
face. That was the end. I exercised and ate properly
and in a little while I weighed 250 pounds.
Then what happened?
I went to the beach and a 350-pound bully kicked
sand in my face.

So I walked up to him and said, "Only a coward
would hit a woman. Why don't you hit a man?"
Then what happened?
That's all I remember.

My mother has the worst memory.
Forgets everything, eh?
No, remembers everything.

I'm sure I met you somewhere.
 That's possible. I've been there a lot lately.

I don't think I caught your name.
 I don't think I dropped it.

Eddie Jones, I haven't seen you in years. You've really changed. You used to be tall and now you're short. You used to be fat and now you're skinny, and your hair is all different.
 Listen, mister, my name's not Eddie Jones; it's Paul Smith.
Oh, you've changed your name too!

SON: Our neighbors must be very poor.
MOTHER: Why do you say that?
SON: You should have seen the fuss they made when their baby swallowed a dime.

My upstairs neighbors are so loud. Last night they kept banging on the floor all night.
 Did they wake you?
No, fortunately I was playing my tuba.

I can trace my ancestors back to Columbus.
 Wow! To 1492?
No, to Ohio.

My grandfather was a famous politician.
 What did he run for?
The border.

Did you have any trouble with your Spanish when you were in Mexico?

No, but the Mexican people did.

I paid over $2,000 to get my baldness cured.

That's a lot of money.

Yes, but it's better to give than recede.

BARBER: Your hair is getting thin.

CUSTOMER: Who wants fat hair?

I heard about a man who invented a hair tonic that can grow hair on a bowling ball.

Did he make a lot of money?

No, no one wants hairy bowling balls.

What's your business?
  Bowling.
How do you like it?
  It's right up my alley.

Do you like soccer?
  Yes, I get a kick out of it.

I'm going jogging, but first I have to stretch my legs.
  Why? Are they too short?

PATIENT: Doctor, I can't sleep at night. I get irritable and can't get along with my brother.
DOCTOR: Try jogging 10 miles every morning.
(Ten days pass.)
PATIENT: Doc, I feel great. I can sleep again and I'm not irritable.
DOCTOR: Great. But how are you getting along with your brother?
PATIENT: How should I know. I'm 100 miles from home.

5. Merrily We Roll Along

I just finished a long run on Broadway.
Really, what play were you in?
What play? A mugger chased me for 20 blocks.

POLICEMAN: Hey, you! What are you doing walking
down the street with a desk on your back and a
computer under your arm?
MAN: I'm impersonating an office, sir.

SHERIFF: Men, I want all of you to be on the
lookout for a man wearing a paper hat, paper
pants and a paper shirt.
DEPUTIES: What is he wanted for?
SHERIFF: Rustling.

Scientists believe that cavemen made the first music by banging stones together.

Gee, I guess that was the first rock music.

Can you carry a tune?

Of course.

Good, then carry the one you're singing and bury it in the backyard.

Do you like music?

Sure, I have a zither at home.

Really, I have a brother.

No, you don't understand. A zither is a kind of lyre.

Well, my brother is, too.

How do you think I played the trumpet?
You really blew it.

It seems as if I'm always breaking into song.
You wouldn't have to break in if you found the right key.

ORCHESTRA CONDUCTOR: I'm surprised that a cow would ask for a job with my orchestra. What instrument do you play?
COW: The bull horn.

Why are you singing to your baby?
I'm trying to get the baby to sleep.
If I were that baby, I'd pretend to sleep already.

Where can I get hold of your sister?
I don't know. She's ticklish.

My sister has a great way to make a quick breakfast.
What's that?
She puts popcorn in the pancakes so they flip themselves over.

What's more useful after it's broken?
I don't know.
An egg.

What side of a cake is the right side.
I don't know.
The side that gets eaten because the other side is left.

TOM SWIFTIES

"This cookie is falling apart," said Tom, feeling crumby.

"Nobody lives in that house," said Tom vacantly.

"Draw an X," said Tom crossly.

"You can sleep in the attic," said Tom loftily.

My foot falls asleep and keeps me awake.
If you're foot falls asleep, how does it keep you awake?
It snores.

Do you snore?
Yes, I sleep soundly.

Mom, my bed is too short.
Then don't sleep so long.

Last night I couldn't get to sleep so I started counting sheep. I got to 25,000.
Then did you get to sleep?
No, then it was time to get up.

What time is it?
I'm not sure, but it's not five o'clock yet.
How do you know?
Because my mother said to be home by 5 o'clock and I'm not home yet.

This clock will run for 30 days without winding.
That's great. How long will it run if you wind it?

Is your watch running?
It sure is.
When is it coming back?

I heard something this morning that opened my eyes.
What was it?
My alarm clock.

Remember that alarm clock you gave me?
Yes.
I had to take it back. It kept waking me up when I was sleeping.

I just got an actor's alarm clock.
  An actor's alarm clock? What's that?
It doesn't ring, it applauds.

DIRECTOR: Now in this scene you jump off the cliff.
ACTOR: But suppose I get killed?
DIRECTOR: Don't worry, it's the last scene in the film.

AGENT TO WRITER: I've got good news and bad
  news for you.
WRITER: What's the good news?
AGENT: Paramount loved your story, absolutely ate
  it up.
WRITER: What's the bad news?
AGENT: Paramount is my cocker spaniel.

Why does your dog carry that bone in its mouth?
  Because its pocket is ripped.

My dog hides under the bed when she hears
thunder and lightning.
  What's wrong with that?
There isn't room for me.

How do you like my new dog?
  Spitz?
No, but he drools a lot.

A man was riding his horse down a bridle path
when a dog walking down the path said, "Hello."
  Surprised, the man said, "I didn't know dogs could talk!"
The horse said, "Neither did I."

FIRST COWBOY: My leg got hurt when I was thrown from a horse.

SECOND COWBOY: I twisted my arm trying to rope a steer.

THIRD COWBOY: I got the worst injury of all. I burned my bottom.

OTHER COWBOYS: How did you do that?

THIRD COWBOY: I tried to ride the range and it was still on.

MOTORIST: How far is it to the next town?

FARMER: Two miles, as the crow flies.

MOTORIST: How far is it if the crow has to roll a flat tire?

I know why your car has a flat tire.

Why?

There was a fork in the road.

DRIVER: I had an accident. My car got stuck in quicksand.

INSURANCE AGENT: Don't get excited.

DRIVER: Why not?

AGENT: Because your car will be completely covered.

WARPED WISE MAN

Why do they call it a speed bump when you have to slow down to get over it?

6. Grin & Bear It

MARTIAN LANDING ON EARTH: Take me to your leader.

YOUNG BOY: I can't.

MARTIAN: Why? Are you frozen with fear?

BOY: No, your spaceship is on my foot.

What part of the horror movies scares you the most?
The part when I run out of popcorn.

Lady, you can't take that dog into the movies. It's not permitted.
That's ridiculous. What harm could a movie do to a little dog?

Did you hear about the Alaskan version of "The Wizard of Oz?"

No, what's it called?

"There's No Place Like Nome."

I have an uncle in Alaska.

Nome?

Of course I know him.

I mean Nome in Alaska.

Of course. I'd know him anywhere.

My daughter went on a cruise.

Jamaica?

No, she wanted to go.

My son came to visit me on vacation.

How nice. Did you meet him at the airport?

No, I've known him all my life.

PASSENGER: What kind of hobbies do they have on airplanes?

PILOT: Air crafts.

Why are airports always so far from town?

Because they want them out where the planes are.

NEWS BULLETIN

Two prisoners escaped from jail yesterday. One is 6'6" and the other is 4'8". Police are looking high and low for them.

ROBBER: This is a holdup! Give me all your money or else!

LADY: Or else what?

ROBBER: Don't confuse me. This is my first job.

Were you afraid when the robber pulled a knife on you?

No, I could see he wasn't a professional. The knife still had butter on it.

JEWELER: Hello, 911. I own a jewelry store and an elephant walked in and sucked up all my jewelry with his trunk and ran away.

POLICE: Can you give me a description?

JEWELER: I can't really, because he had a nylon stocking over his head.

CAMEL 1: How is life treating you?
CAMEL 2: I've had hard times, but I'm finally
getting over the hump.

I was arrested at the zoo yesterday.
Arrested! For what?
Feeding the pigeons.
But, what's wrong with that?
I was feeding them to the lions.

What do raccoons eat?
They eat anything.
But what if they can't find anything?
Then they eat something else.

Did you hear the joke about the squirrel? It's nutty.

FARMER: Young man, what are you doing up my
chestnut tree?
YOUNG MAN: Nuttin'.

FARMER: What are you doing up my apple tree?
BOY: Well, one of the apples fell off and I was
trying to put it back.

Did you hear about the farmer whose tractor got
stuck in reverse?
No, what happened?
He unplowed five acres.

Did you hear about the graffiti artist who retired
because he saw the handwriting on the wall?

PERVERTED PROVERB

To err is human; to cover it up is too.

PASSENGER: Operator, take me to the sixth floor.

ELEVATOR OPERATOR: I'm sorry, sir, but this building only has five stories.

PASSENGER: Okay, then take me to the third floor twice.

HOMEOWNER: What's wrong with my kitchen faucet?

PLUMBER: It's out of sink.

MOM: For once I'd like to come into the kitchen and not see you digging through the refrigerator.

SON: Try whistling before you come in.

Did you know my robot can walk?
That's nothing. My refrigerator can run.

MOTHER: The only reason I'm grounding you is because I love you.
DAUGHTER: I'm sure glad you don't hate me.

MOTHER (*spanking her child*): This is going to hurt me more than it hurts you.
SON: I guess you've had enough then.

If you misbehave again I may have to spank you.
Dad, when you were a boy did your father spank you?
Yes, he did.
And when Grandpa was bad, did his father spank him?
Yes.
Well, don't you think it's about time we tried to overcome this inherited cruelty?

TOURIST: This is a steep drop-off. Why don't you put up a fence and danger sign?

RESIDENT: We did have a sign once, but nobody fell off, so we took it down.

Didn't you used to have two windmills in town? What happened? One of them is missing.

They tore it down. There wasn't enough wind for two.

This lightning scares me.

Don't worry, it will be over in a flash.

There is one good thing about smog.

What's that?

You can see what you're breathing.

They say London is the foggiest city.

I've been someplace foggier.

Where's that?

I don't know. It was too foggy to tell.

Why is your head sticking through that hole in the umbrella?

So I can see if it stopped raining.

The trouble with you is that you're always wishing for things you haven't got.

What else is there to wish for?

If you had one wish, what would you wish for?

A mountain of gold.

Would you give me half?

Certainly not! Wish for your own mountain.

FERD: Don't you wish life was like television?

NERD: I can't answer that now.

FERD: Why?

NERD: I'm on a commercial break.

TV REPAIRMAN: What seems to be the trouble with your TV, ma'am?

WOMAN: It seems to have double images. I hope you men can fix it.

How come you have three pairs of glasses?
One is for driving, the second is for reading and the third is for looking for the other two.

Did you know that eagles have such keen eyesight they can read a newspaper from a mile away?
Wow! I didn't even know they could read.

My mother does bird imitations.
Really? How does she do that?
She watches me like a hawk.

ACTOR: I do bird imitations.

PRODUCER: I can't use you. I've seen hundreds of bird imitators.

ACTOR: Okay. Is it all right if I fly out the window?

PERVERTED PROVERB

A bird in the hand is not good table manners.

7. Jester Minute

How long will your brother be in jail?
Thirty days.
What's the charge?
No charge. Everything's free.

PRISON WARDEN: I'm sorry, but we've kept you a week too long.
CONVICT: That's okay. You can take it off my time the next time I come in.

PREACHER: In times of trial what brings us the greatest comfort?
MAN: An acquittal.

These cookies taste terrible. Did you follow the recipe correctly? Three cups of flour, a dash of salt, etc.
A dash of salt? I thought it said a dish of salt!

Would you like some of my chocolate candy?
Yes, thank you.
The ones with the teeth marks have hard centers.

MOM: Be careful and don't drop that cookie.
DAUGHTER: Why?
MOTHER: Because chocolate chips.

My daughter is impossible. She keeps asking me for money. Last week it was $20. Yesterday it was $10 and today it's $15.
What does she do with it all?
I don't know. I don't give it to her.

Dad, could I have a dollar?
When I was your age I asked for cents.
Okay, give me 100 cents.

TEENAGE SON: Dad, do you think in time I'll be able to stand on my own feet?
FATHER: I certainly do.
TEENAGER: Well, I can't on the allowance I get now.

MILLIONAIRE: When I came to this city I only had one dollar with which to make my way.
TV INTERVIEWER: I suppose you spent it wisely.
MILLIONAIRE: I certainly did. I used it to telegraph home for money.

TOM
SWIFTIES

"I don't want to go to jail," said Tom with conviction.

"I'd like to return this sweater," Tom said sheepishly.

"I hate chemistry," Tom said acidly.

"I like fresh pastry," said Tom tartly.

I lost 20 pounds in England last summer.
How much is that in American money?

Why is paper money more valuable than coins?
I don't know, why?
When you put it in your pocket you double it and when you take it out you find it in creases.

I know a couple who talk in their sleep. He plays golf and she goes to auctions.
Really?
Yes. Just the other night he yelled, "Fore!" and she yelled, "Four-fifty!"

CUSTOMER: I'd like to buy some sealing wax.
STORE CLERK: You've got to be kidding. Who'd want to wax a ceiling?

Where did you buy your goose-feather comforter?
Down town.

I've finally perfected my duck call.
  Let's hear it.
Here ducky, ducky, ducky!

FARMER: Son, baby pigs are called piglets.
SON: Then baby bulls must be called bullets and
  baby chickens chicklets.

Did your pig break her pen?
  Yes, now she has to type her letters.

MOTHER PIG: Why do you want to become a
  football when you grow up?
PIGLET: So they'll be sure to pass me when I go to
  school.

DINER: I haven't come to any ham in my ham
  sandwich.
WAITER: Take another bite.
DINER: Still no ham.
WAITER: You must have eaten right by it.

A college student wrote
  his father a note that
  said:
  No money.
  Not funny.
  Love, Sonny.
His father wrote back:
  So sad.
  Too bad.
  Love, Dad.

PATRON: This steak you brought me is rare. I said "well done"!
WAITRESS: Thank you, sir. I don't get many compliments.

CUSTOMER: You call this beef-noodle soup your special? I can't find any beef or noodles in it.
WAITER: That's why it's special.

DINER: Miss, this potato is bad.
WAITRESS: Bad, bad, potato! Now if that potato gives you any more trouble, you just let me know.

 **WARPED WISE MAN**

Money can't buy you happiness but it can pay the rent when you're miserable.

GIRL: I want potatoes with lots of eyes.
FOOD STORE CLERK: Why do you want lots of eyes?
GIRL: Because Mom says they're going to have to see us through the week.

MOTHER: Please go to the store and get me some tomato paste.
SON: Why? Are the tomatoes broken?

CUSTOMER: The banana I bought here yesterday was green and hard to peel.
GROCER: What did you expect at sales prices, a zipper?

BOY IN CANDY STORE: Give me an all-day sucker.
CLERK: Here you are.
BOY: Looks kind of small.
CLERK: Yeah, the days are getting shorter.

I'd like to purchase a pound of nails.
   That will be two dollars plus tax.
I don't want tacks, just nails.

CUSTOMER: Do you have any thumbtacks?
CLERK: No, but I've got some fingernails.

PATIENT: Doctor, I think I have too much iron in
   my diet.
DOCTOR: Why do you think that?
PATIENT: Because I have nails growing out of the
   tips of my fingers.

PATIENT: I just can't seem to shake this cold. I spent the last seven days in bed and I feel drained.

DOCTOR: Well, that's the problem. Don't you know that seven days in bed makes one weak?

NEWS BULLETIN

A man walked into a hospital and asked for a brain transplant. Fortunately the doctors were able to change his mind.

DOCTOR: I've given you a thorough exam and all you need is a rest.

PATIENT: But, I feel sick. Why don't you look at my tongue?

DOCTOR: That needs a rest too.

DOCTOR: Don't you know that my hours are from 2 P.M. to 4 P.M?

PATIENT: Yes, but the dog that bit me didn't.

I lost my pants while running.
   Were they loose?
No, but the neighbor's dog was.

Would you like to pet my new dog?
   I don't know. I heard him barking and growling. Does he bite?
That's what I want to find out.

Why is your dog sitting in the corner?

Because he's been a bad little doggie.

What did he do?

Yesterday he was expelled from obedience school.

There are three reasons people have dogs for pets.

What are they?

Hyenas are too noisy. Elephants can't fit through the front door and you can't walk a fish on a leash.

Young man, there is no fishing here.

You're telling me! I haven't caught anything in two hours.

MAN TO BOY FISHING: How many fish have you caught?

BOY: Well, if I catch this one and two more I'll have three.

YOUNG MAN: How many fish have you caught, mister?

FISHERMAN: None yet. But I've only been fishing for an hour.

YOUNG MAN: That's better than the man did yesterday.

FISHERMAN: How's it better?

YOUNG MAN: It took him five hours to do what you did in one.

GUIDE: I never guide hunters anymore, just
    fishermen.
HUNTER: Why?
GUIDE: I've never been mistaken for a fish.

What's wrong?
I bought a camouflage tent.
What's wrong with that?
I can't find it.

CAMPER: What does it mean if I can look up at the
    stars?
OTHER CAMPER: It probably means someone stole
    your tent.

What do you call a campsite trampled by thousands
of tiny insects?
I have no idea, what?
A gnatural disaster.

Do ants have brains?
*Of course they do. How do you think they always know
when you're having a picnic?*

CENTIPEDE: You're stepping on my foot.
ANT: Which one?

SPIDER: I'm sorry I'm late for lunch, but I was
    answering my e-mail.
OTHER SPIDER: You get e-mail. How come?
SPIDER: Simple. I'm on the web.

SPIDER: Will you share your curds with me?
MISS MUFFET: No whey.

What happened after Old King Cole ordered his
men to mix chopped cabbage with mayonnaise?
  What happened?
It became known as Cole's Law.

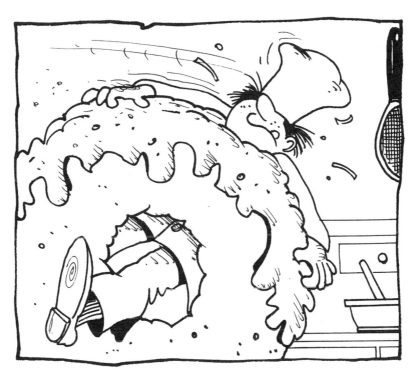

8. Hardy Ha-Ha's

I'm the new manager of the doughnut shop.
  Are you in charge of everything?
Yes, the hole works.

CUSTOMER: What do you do with the leftover holes
  in your doughnuts?
BAKER: We tie them together with string and make
  fishnets out of them.

CUSTOMER: Could I have some bread?
BAKER: No, I knead it.

MOTHER: Did I make the toast too dark?
DAUGHTER: I can't tell yet. The smoke is too thick.

PEANUT: Would you go out with me?
CASHEW: Are you nuts?

I've got my boyfriend to the point where he eats
out of my hand.
   Saves a lot of dishwashing, doesn't it?

I hear you broke off your engagement. What
happened?
   Oh, it's just that my feeling for him changed.
Are you returning the ring?
   Oh, no. My feeling for the ring hasn't changed.

Did you hear that Harry got married?
   *Yeah, he spent so much money on his girl he decided to
   marry her for his money.*

How come you broke up with your girlfriend?
   She started using four-letter words.
Like what?
   Like "Find some work."

GIRL: I'll have to give you your engagement ring
   back. I can't marry you. I love someone else.
BOY: Who is he?
GIRL: Why? Are you going to beat him up?
BOY: No, I'm going to sell him an engagement ring
   real cheap.

Did you hear the joke about the cheap boomerang?
You never get it back.

You say you live off the spat of the land. Don't you
mean the fat of the land?
  No, I'm a marriage counselor.

MIDDLE-AGED WOMAN: I just got married because I
  didn't want to wind up an old maid.
DOCTOR: Okay, bring her in and I'll wind her up
  for you.

Doc, before I get married there's one thing I have
to get off my chest.
  What's that?
The tattooed heart with the name "Mary" on it.

I went to a wedding where a man married 16 wives.
How could he marry 16 wives?
He married 4 richer, 4 poorer, 4 better or 4 worse.

Where should we meet?
Under the clothesline, that's where I hang out.

Can you tie up the loose ends?
Knot possible.

WARPED WISE MAN

Don't procrastinate now, do it later.

How's your son you took into business with you?
He's amazing. He's only been with me for two weeks and he's already a month behind in his work.

MANAGER: You're 30 minutes late. Don't you know what time we start here?
OFFICE BOY: No, by the time I get here everyone is already working.

BOSS: You certainly ask for a big salary for a man with no experience.
JOB APPLICANT: Yes, but it's much harder work when you don't know what you're doing.

BOSS: Before I hire you I have to ask you, do you have a previous record?
JOB APPLICANT: No, I've never been caught.

EMPLOYER: You have no experience. Just what kind of job are you looking for?

APPLICANT: I'd like to be an executive. Maybe a vice-president.

EMPLOYER: We already have 12 vice-presidents.

APPLICANT: That's all right. I'm not superstitious.

 WARPED WISE MAN

I thank my lucky stars I'm not superstitious.

FORTUNE-TELLER: You will be unhappy and discontented until you're 40.

CLIENT: And then?

FORTUNE-TELLER: You'll get used to it.

FROG (*telephoning a psychic*): Can you tell me my future?

PSYCHIC: You are going to meet a beautiful girl who will know all about you.

FROG: That's great! Will I meet her at a party?

PSYCHIC: No. Next semester in biology class.

I saw a really bad magician last week.
What was his best trick?
He made the audience disappear.

MAGICIAN: I do one of the greatest tricks of all times. I saw a woman in half.

AGENT: You call that a new trick. Magicians have been doing that for years.

MAGICIAN: Really! Lengthwise?

I'm going to a reincarnation party.
  What's that?
People are supposed to come as they were.

I have an invitation to go to Jane's party but I can't
go.
  Why not?
It says from four to seven and I'm nine.

Why did you push your friend?
  I wanted him to go home.
Why didn't you ask him to leave?
  That wouldn't have been polite.

FIRST SNAKE: I'm writing my hiss-tory.
SECOND SNAKE: I'm a writer too. I write boa-
  graphies.

Look, a green snake!
  *Don't touch it! It might be just as dangerous as a ripe
  one.*

Why does a mink have fur?
  I don't know. Why?
If he didn't, he would be a little bare.

Show me a sneezing polar bear and I'll show you a
perfect snow blower.

Young man, what are you doing up my tree?
  Well, your sign said: "Keep off the grass."

Yesterday I bought three plants. I planted one in my yard, another in my neighbor's yard and the third in my other neighbor's yard.

Why did you do that?

The nursery said to plant them a yard apart.

How did you select your new gardener?

We weeded the others out.

Why are you putting newspapers by your tomato plants?

I heard that if you talk to your plants they grow better.

So, what has that got to do with it?

I don't have time to talk to them, so maybe they'll read.

Is your dog paper-trained?

No, he can't read a thing.

EYE DOCTOR: How many lines can you read on that chart?

PATIENT: What chart?

LADY: Doctor, my husband thinks he's an automobile.

PSYCHIATRIST: Show him into my office.

LADY: I can't. He's double-parked.

DOCTOR: Don't worry, after the operation you'll be a new man.

PATIENT: That's wonderful. Could you send the bill to the old man?

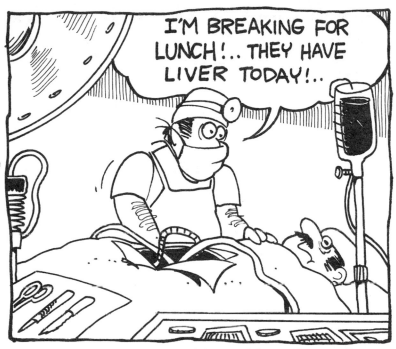

PATIENT: I have this terrible problem, doctor. I keep stealing postage stamps.

DOCTOR: Don't worry. I think I can help you lick it.

CUSTOMER: Postman, do you have a letter for me?

MAIL CARRIER: What's your name?

CUSTOMER: It should be on the letter.

Why are you kicking the mailbox?

I'm taking a correspondence course and we're having a protest demonstration.

Customer service speaking. May I help you?

Yes, I don't want to say your delivery is slow, but the flower seeds I ordered last spring just arrived as a bouquet.

What is this kleptomania I keep hearing about? Is it catching?

No, it's taking.

JUDGE: Do you know the difference between right and wrong?

DEFENDANT: Of course I do.

JUDGE: Then why do you always do wrong?

DEFENDANT: That shows it's not guesswork.

JUDGE: The last time I saw you I told you I didn't want to see you again.

PRISONER: I know. I told that to the policeman but he didn't believe me.

Thanks for trusting me with your secret.

Don't mention it.

9. Giggles & Jiggles

I saw you running alongside your bike this morning.
Yes, I was late and didn't have time to get on.

Did I return your bike last week?
No, you didn't.
Oh, I wanted to borrow it again.

HUSBAND: I didn't forget your birthday. I bought
you this great new mink coat.
WIFE: Yes, dear, but you promised me a new car.
HUSBAND: I know, but I couldn't find anyone
selling imitation autos.

All this talk about backseat driving is a lot of bunk.
I've been driving for 10 years and I never heard a
word from the backseat of my car.

What kind of car do you drive?

A hearse.

Did you know I can read bumper stickers on cars
going 55 miles per hour?

No kidding.

Yeah, I took a speed-reading course.

How much do used batteries cost?

Nothing, they are free of charge.

 **WARPED WISE MAN**

Why do people park in a driveway and
drive on a parkway?

My coat is frayed.

'Fraid of what?

What should I wear with my new tie?

A beard.

JUDGE: Lady, have you ever been a witness in a suit
like this?

LADY: No, the last time I was here I had on a blue
outfit.

CUSTOMER: Look at this coat you sold me! It split up the back.

STORE CLERK: That shows how tightly the buttons were sewed on.

Did you knit this sweater all by yourself?
Yes, all except the hole you put your head through. That was there when I started.

Have you forgotten you owe me five dollars?
No, but give me time and I will.

You remind me of Joe.
Why? Do we look alike?
Not in the least. You both owe me five dollars.

Lend me five dollars.
I only have four.
Okay. Lend me the four and you'll owe me one.

NEWS BULLETIN

The local cemetery raised
its prices and blamed the high cost of living.

Do you like moving pictures?
Yes, I do.
Good. Help me move some pictures to the other
room.

WOMAN AT THE MOVIES: If my hat prevents you
   from seeing the movies, let me know and I can
   take it off.
MAN BEHIND HER: Don't bother. Your hat is funnier
   than the movie.

BEGGAR: Lady, could you help me? It's cold and
   snowy out and I've eaten nothing but snow for
   the last three days.
LADY: You're lucky. What if it were summer?

HOUSEWIFE: You should be ashamed of yourself to
   be seen begging at my house.
TRAMP: Oh, don't feel bad. I've seen worse houses
   than this one.

LADY: Are you satisfied spending all your time walking around the country begging?

HOBO: No, madam, I wish I had a car.

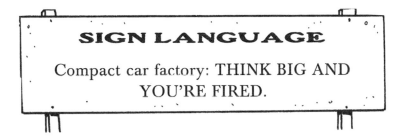

SIGN LANGUAGE

Compact car factory: THINK BIG AND YOU'RE FIRED.

TRAVELER: Is this the bus to California?

TICKET AGENT: Yes, it goes to California in 10 minutes.

TRAVELER: Wow! That fast!

I'm always sick the night before a trip.
Then why don't you leave a day earlier?

PASSENGER: Are you sure this train stops at San Francisco?

CONDUCTOR: If it doesn't, you're going to hear an awful splash.

FOOTBALL COACH: Jackson, get in there.

PLAYER: But, coach, I can't play today. I broke my leg.

COACH: That's a lame excuse.

BASEBALL COACH: What do you get when you reach third base?

PLAYER: A triple.

COACH: Right. And what do you get when you hit one over the fence?

PLAYER: A new ball.

BASEBALL COACH: Remember all those batting tips and fielding tips I gave you?

ROOKIE: I sure do.

COACH: Well, forget them. We traded you.

I'm a very famous speaker. I spoke at Yankee Stadium to thousands of people.

Really! What did you say?

Peanuts, popcorn, cold drinks.

CUSTOMER: Could I put this wallpaper on myself?

CLERK: Sure, but it would look better on the wall.

BOOKS NEVER WRITTEN

How to Play Basketball by Duncan Pass.

That Ain't All by Morris Cumming.

How to Catch Worms by Earl E. Byrd.

Cutting Down Trees by Shane Saw.

SALESMAN: May I choose a fence for you?

CUSTOMER: Okay, you picket.

SIGN LANGUAGE

Convenience store: WE'LL SERVE YOU FAST NO MATTER HOW LONG IT TAKES.

Let's go to that restaurant, "The Budapest."
No thanks, not Hungary.

DINER: I heard that scientists say that we are what
we eat.
OTHER DINER: Oh, let's order something rich.

Why did you give that hat check girl a $5 tip?
Look at the great-looking hat she gave me.

Why are you upset?
*I saw a sign in the restaurant that said "Watch Your
Coat and Hat," so I did and someone stole my dinner.*

PATRON (*in restaurant*): What are you doing?
OTHER PATRON: I'm watching my coat.
PATRON: Would you stop watching the coats and
eat your dinner!
OTHER PATRON: I'm only watching my coat. Yours
disappeared a half-hour ago.

Is that your dog?
Yes, he was a pointer, but my mother ruined him.
How did she do that?
She taught him that it wasn't polite to point.

I'd like to buy a sweater for my dog.
What size?
I have no idea.
Why don't you bring him in and have him try one on?
I can't do that. It's a surprise.

You say you have a carpenter dog. I never heard of that kind.

Yes, just yesterday it made a bolt for the door.

I have to get rid of this dachshund.

How come?

It takes him so long to get in the door he lets all the flies in.

My uncle once shot a deer in his pajamas.

How did the deer get into your uncle's pajamas?

We're lost in the woods. Shoot three shots in the air.

Okay.

No one came. You'd better shoot three more.

Okay, but I hope someone comes soon. We're almost out of arrows.

PATIENT: Doctor, you've got to help me. Everyone thinks I'm a liar.
DOCTOR: I can't believe that.

Doctor, I feel funny today. What should I do?
Become a comedian.

Doctor, I think I'm a pin.
I see your point.

JUDGE: Remember, you are under oath. How old are you?
WOMAN: Twenty-one and some months.
JUDGE: How many months?
WOMAN: One hundred and twenty-eight.

JUDGE: Why couldn't you settle this matter out of court?
DEFENDANT: We tried to, Your Honor, but the cops broke it up.

Do you believe in capital punishment?
Only if it's not too severe.

JUDGE: You are charged with selling eternal youth pills.
MEDICINE MAN: Yes, your honor.
JUDGE: Have you ever been arrested on this charge before?
MEDICINE MAN: Yes, twice. Once in 1843 and again in 1912.

CAMPER: How about sleeping on the top bunk
    tonight?
OTHER CAMPER: Nah, I don't like to oversleep.

CAMPER: There's a large leak over my bunk.
COUNSELOR: That's what it said in the ad.
CAMPER: What?
COUNSELOR: Running water in every room.

Are you going to the hiker's meeting tonight?
    No, I can't get a ride.

CAMP LEADER: Why do you only carry one log at a
    time from here while all the others carry two?
CAMPER: I guess the others are too lazy to make two
    trips.

BARBER: Sir, would you mind turning the other side of your face toward me?

CUSTOMER: Why, are you through shaving this side?

BARBER: No, I can't stand the sight of blood.

REPORTER: Is your job dangerous?

BARBER: I have a lot of close shaves, but mostly I get out of scrapes.

10. Don't Be Silly

FLIGHT ATTENDANT: I'm handing out gum before the flight starts. It will prevent your ears from popping as we climb.

After the flight everyone left except one man. "Why are you still here?" she asked.

"'Ah, you have to speak up," he yelled. "I can't hear you with this gum in my ears."

PILOT TO PASSENGER: We have good news and bad
    news. The bad news is we're lost.
PASSENGER: What's the good news?
PILOT: We're making good time.

PILOT: We have lost one of our engines so we'll be an hour late for our arrival.

PILOT *(later)*: We just lost another engine so we'll be three hours late for our arrival.

PASSENGER: If the last engine dies, we'll be up here forever.

GOLFER: Caddy, how would you have played that last shot?

CADDY: Under an assumed name.

MAN ON GOLF COURSE: Before I hire you, caddy, tell me, are you good at finding lost golf balls?

CADDY: Yes sir, I'm the best.

GOLFER: Great! You're hired. Now go out and find us some golf balls so we can start the game.

FIRST GOLFER: How's our game?

SECOND GOLFER: I shoot in the 70's. When it gets colder I quit.

Are Jim's feet big?
I don't know. I never saw him with his shoes off.

How much are your $20 shoes?
Ten dollars a foot.

CUSTOMER: These shoes are too narrow and too pointed for me.

CLERK: That's the way they're wearing them this year.

CUSTOMER: Yes, but I'm wearing last year's feet.

Why don't you soak your sore feet in hot water?
What? And get my shoes wet?

NEWS BULLETIN

A shoe factory downsized and
gave all its employees the boot.

WAITER: I recommend the fish. It's been our
specialty for years.
PATRON: Well, bring me something you haven't had
for so long.

CUSTOMER: Waiter, this soup tastes funny.
WAITER: Then why aren't you laughing?

COULD YOU DO MY BACK?!!.

Waiter, there's a rubber band in my soup.
Well, you told me to make it snappy.

CUSTOMER: Miss, you have your finger in my soup.
WAITRESS: That's all right, it's not hot.

How was that new restaurant you ate in?
*It's terrible. It's so bad they can't give out doggy bags
because it would be cruelty to animals.*

Why do fire trucks have dogs on them?
To find the fire hydrant.

MAN: Are you sure this dog you're selling me is
     loyal?
OWNER: He sure is. I sold him five times and every
       time he's come back.

My dog is going to obedience school.
That's expensive. How can you afford it?
He won a collarship.

How much is that big dog?
Fifty dollars.
And how much is that tiny dog?
One hundred dollars.
And how much would it be if I bought no dog at
all?

We have a new dog.
What's he like?
Anything we feed him.

HUNTER: Look! Here's some bear tracks.
SECOND HUNTER: Good. I'll go see where he came from and you go see where he went.

See that bear rug on the floor. That bear was only six feet away when I shot him. It was either him or me.
Well, the bear certainly makes a better rug.

Did you hear about the hunter who had an accident?
No, what happened?
It seems he saw some tracks. He went to study them closely. That's when the train hit him.

Did you hear that the explosive expert died?
Yes, may he rest in pieces.

LAWYER: I've come to help you with your damages.
CLIENT: I've got all the damages I need. I need repairs.

Did you hear about the fire at the soap factory?
No, was anybody hurt?
No, they all slid down the lather.

My brother can run the hundred-yard dash in six seconds.
That's impossible. The world record is nine seconds.
My brother knows a shortcut.

I had a fight with my brother last night. When it was over he crawled on his hands and knees.
What did he say?
Come out from under that bed, you coward!

I'd like to talk to your mother, young man. Is she engaged?
Engaged? She's married.

SON: I want to be an accountant when I grow up.
FATHER: Go figure.

Why does it take longer to find your dad than your mom?
Because he's farther.

DOCTOR: Have you been taking those memory pills
I gave you?
PATIENT: No, I forgot to take them.

DOCTOR: How is the man who swallowed the
spoon?
NURSE: He can hardly stir.

What's wrong?
*The doctor gave me some medicine and told me to take
three teaspoons a day.*
So?
I only have two teaspoons.

Does your doctor make house calls?
Yes, but your house has to be very sick.

Someone picked my pocket.
What did he get?
Practice.

Hey, what are you doing with your hands in my pockets!
I'm making change and I didn't want to bother you.

FIRST BURGLAR: I need glasses.
SECOND BURGLAR: What makes you think that?
FIRST BURGLAR: Last week when I turned the knobs on the safe, music came out.

EXHAUSTED HIKER: Am I glad to see you! I've been lost for two days.
OTHER HIKER: Don't get excited. I'm been lost for two weeks.

HIKER: Are we lost?
GUIDE: Of course not. We're here. It's the trail that's lost.

Do you know where we are?
Yes.
Where?
Lost.

DAD: Where do you want to go this summer?
SON: Somewhere I haven't been in months.
DAD: How about the barber shop?

90

BARBER: How would you like your hair cut?
YOUNG MAN: I'd like to keep my hair long.
BARBER: Don't worry. You'll have it for a while yet.

MAN: I don't like the looks of this haircut.
BARBER: Don't worry. It will grow on you.

I can't decide if I should become a barber or write
short stories.
   Flip a coin: Heads or tails.

BOYFRIEND: If I give you a quarter will you give me
   a lock of your sister's hair?
KID BROTHER: Give me a dollar and I'll give you
   the whole wig.

Are you paid weekly?
   Yes, very weakly.

Hello, I'm a chimney sweep and I'd like to know if I can clean your chimney?

No, I clean it myself.

O.K. Soot yourself.

WIFE: What's the matter, dear?

HUSBAND: You know those aptitude tests we give our employees.

WIFE: Yes.

HUSBAND: Well, I took one today and it's a good thing I own the company.

REPORTER: I understand you're going to retire after building one more canal.

ENGINEER: Yes, it will be a last-ditch effort.

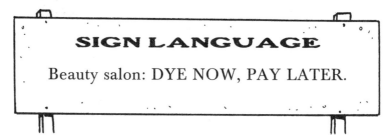

SIGN LANGUAGE

Beauty salon: DYE NOW, PAY LATER.

BEGGAR: Mister, could I have $1,000 for a cup of coffee?

STARTLED MAN: $1,000! How many people do you think are going to give you $1,000?

BEGGAR: If only a few do, I could stop begging.

BEGGAR: Could you give me $1 for a cup of coffee?

MAN ON STREET: But coffee is only 50 cents.

BEGGAR: Yes, but I'm a big tipper.

BEGGAR: Could you lend me $150 for a cup of coffee?

LADY: But coffee is only 50 cents.

BEGGAR: You expect me to walk into a restaurant dressed like this?

Can you spare a dollar for a piece of cake?

Cake? Most people ask for bread.

Today's my birthday.

SERGEANT: Why didn't you stop when I yelled, "Company, halt?"

RECRUIT: Well, I've been here for six weeks and I didn't think I was company anymore.

I'd like to speak to the general.
   I'm sorry, but the general is sick today.
What made him sick?
   Oh, things in general.

Did the Confederate troops obey their
commanders?
   Generally.

That joke was so bad we had to put it at the end of
the book.

ABOUT THE AUTHOR

Charles Keller has been working and playing with comedy all his life. Working for CBS as a script consultant, he edited many of the great classic sitcoms, such as *M*A*S*H, All in the Family,* and *The Mary Tyler Moore Show,* and he also worked on other prime-time comedy shows. He got started writing children's books because he didn't like many of the ones he read and thought he could do better. Now, over 40 books later, he maintains the country's largest archive of children's rhymes, riddles, witty sayings, and jokes, and constantly updates his massive collection. When he isn't writing children's books, he can be found creating educational software for children. Born in New York, Charles Keller is a graduate of St. Peter's College. He presently resides in Union City, Jersey.

ABOUT THE ILLUSTRATOR

Jeff Sinclair has been drawing cartoons ever since he could hold a pen. He has won several local and national awards for cartooning and humorous illustration. When he is not at his drawing board, he can be found renovating his house and working on a water garden in the backyard. Jeff lives in Vancouver, British Columbia, Canada, with his wife, Karen, son, Brennan, daughter, Conner, and golden Lab, Molly.